trust

Moving forward when you
don't have all the answers

trust

Moving forward when you
don't have all the answers

Stefanny Kerr

INTRODUCTION

I am so glad you're here. I'm honored that you are taking a moment out of your day to stop and engage with the words presented. I've prayed for you, and I truly believe you will hear every whisper that's intended for you. So, welcome. You are at home.

Each chapter in this book details a phase in the process of healing, growth, and discovery I personally went through with God. First, God asked me to trust Him. There is no way the average person will go on a journey with someone they don't trust. Time and time again, as I was beginning this process, God would ask, extending His hand towards me as I faced the unknown, "Do you trust me?" As I began to trust my teacher, I opened myself up to learning and un-learning—both very necessary steps in the lifelong passage to becoming who God has called us to be. And, ultimately, to support us in returning to His original plan for our lives.

As we go through life, we pick up many beliefs that completely hinder our progress and interfere with a correct self-perception. This could be as seemingly simple as believing we are unwanted after having not been chosen for a school team or concluding there must be something inherently wrong with us because of the amount of pain we have endured in our lives. The issue then becomes how we view and understand ourselves. When we wrongfully see ourselves, we accept less than we deserve. We stay longer in situations that we know we should leave, and we operate in self-sabotage when we could be walking in destiny and purpose. During this time of trusting, learning, feeling, growing, examining, and evolving, I didn't even realize ALL of that was taking place! I was just living my life the best way I knew how. The relationship between trusting God and the very real resistance we sometimes feel emotionally is a constant battle. Our emotions, as valid as they may be, do not define God. Nor do they determine how trustworthy He is and whether we should move forward in obedience or not.

It was not always an easy process of trusting what often made no sense, to me. Like a rollercoaster, I felt every emotion. Every high and every low, every twist and every turn. I couldn't understand why He would ask me to quit my job when I had no other job or business at the time. But I trusted Him, so I left my job. I personally could not see why certain relationships needed to end, but I trusted Him, so I ended them. God sees everything we cannot see. He knows what we simply could not.

As I learned to hear His instruction and follow it, I began to see a blessed path laid out before me. I began to heal. As I took God's hand and walked with Him forward, every area of my life began to look more fruitful than it had before: physically, spiritually, emotionally, and relationally. Everything shifted for the better when I began trusting the process my teacher was leading me through. For me, this fruitfulness took the form of physical and relational healing. I didn't realize it at the time, but the excruciatingly painful eczema that had 'suddenly appeared' was a sign of a broken internal relationship with myself and others. I had let so many people walk all over me.

Interestingly enough, when the eczema got really bad, I couldn't walk. For me, physical healing was a process that took years and is one I am still navigating. For you, the process of restoration may be an internal one, such as learning to forgive yourself or perhaps standing in your truth and in your power. Whatever that may look like for you, believe me when I say whatever journey God is inviting you on will be worth any moments of uncertainty you felt at the beginning. I know how you feel. I felt scared. At times unsure. But here's what I found: any journey with God will always restore, and it will always heal.

HOW TO READ
THIS BOOK

As I began to write this book, I realized that although these were chapters in the story God was writing concerning my life, they were also chapters in the lives of many women I knew. With this realization, I felt the book needed to evolve. I wouldn't simply tell my story, but I would share my experiences while weaving in the realities of lives around me. Each chapter begins with my thoughts on that particular phase of the process. Next, I introduce you to a character through narration and then finally into a glimpse of their lives as told in a short story. All of these stories have been inspired by real women and real events. As you read, I hope you are encouraged to know that you are not alone. Of course, every person's story is unique to them. But whether you realize it or not, so many other people have seen what you've seen and have allowed the best teacher there ever was to invite them on a journey of healing, discovery, and growth. Having done so, they found that their decision to follow Him was the best decision they could ever have made. You too, can go from wondering if you can trust Him to knowing you always can. God wants you to become the most powerful version of yourself, reflecting back to Him the investment of love He was always willing to pour out and always will be.

TABLE OF CONTENTS

*This book is dedicated to the ultimate Way Maker and the
One worthy of trusting with my life: God.*

ACKNOWLEDGMENTS

This book would not have been possible without the support of the Beyond The Book Media Family! I am so grateful for the Seven-day Writing Challenge and the Twenty-one Day Bootcamp- both life changers! You all pour so much of your heart into serving at the highest level and making sure every writer's book is released to do the work God intended for it to do! Thank you so much.

Deep appreciation to my Author Bootcamp Afterparty Crew, aka Sister Scribes! God certainly had His hand in how we all met. I love you all.

Thank you to the three amazing ladies who read the very first draft: Nicole, Stephanie, and Teighlor. I appreciate your time and feedback so immensely. You all are world changers, and I am so grateful to know you.

To my family, thank you for your continuous and unfailing support of EVERYTHING I do—Dad, Mom, Lamacorn, Patty, Jay. Aunty and Pops I love you!

Last but not least, sincerest appreciation to my friends. Those who encourage, listen, pray for and celebrate my every project. Life would not be the same without you, and I honor you and your presence. I love you all.

TRUST

Who and what do you trust when everything around you is unstable?

How do you know where to place your foot when the ground is literally moving beneath your feet?

Trust requires a knowing.

A knowing that even if everything around you is falling apart and has been for as long as you can remember, there is one thing that never changes.

One that won't move or be threatened by the weight of your fears.

God.

He doesn't change.

Trust requires a knowing.

An inner knowing that helps you believe in what you know to be true despite what your eyes see.

Selah. Pause. Breathe.

She didn't ask for all the pain. It just, kind of, found her. Like a package, it came delivered in the mail addressed to her. She was too young to understand that when a package arrives and has your name on it, you don't have to open it. Besides, it was opened for her. Enclosed: generational trauma, abuse, confusion, and violence. They all etched themselves on her little soul before she had a chance to be a child.

So, instead of love, she learned anger. As opposed to silence, peace, and calm, she learned violence so loud it would not be ignored. As opposed to joy, she learned how to master the mask. She didn't know, nor could she have, that her experience was not 'normal' that this pain was excessive and cruel, designed to destroy her. But, somehow, she was not destroyed. Her soul had been badly wounded and was in desperate need of real divinely sourced love. But still, somehow, she was not destroyed.

"God is within her, she will not fall; God will help her at break of day" (New International Version, Psalm 46:5).

Trust must be cultivated intentionally.

We trust what we know. Without knowing a thing, it is difficult to place confidence in what it will be or accomplish.

And, in order to know, we must give ourselves permission to be seen in the vulnerable position of needing.

Needing knowledge that we don't yet have.

Needing insight that we haven't yet grasped. But once we know, then we can trust.

We can hold out our hand, with all of the pain held between our fingers, and say, "I didn't know what to do with you when you arrived." But now I know.

I don't have to keep you.

I don't have to embrace you.

I can send you away.

And after you've been sent away, I may still find traces and evidence of the places you have crept into, but even then, I can find you and decide not to welcome you any longer.

Kayla

I don't know if she knew she didn't have to keep the pain. It was such a part of her life that everything seemed like one big tragic play, one scene unfolding after the other, as if on cue. At first, pain chose her. But then, after a while, she chose pain.

She no longer saw herself as worthy of receiving wholesome and healing love. So, she chose the destructive kind. The kind of "love" that kept her up at night, crying and asking herself why she wasn't enough. The kind of "love" that caused her to wonder if his unfaithfulness was her fault and whether his actions would lead to her contracting another disease. The kind of "love" that did not care if she was worried about how the bills would get paid, to the point that she would consider anything, even sex work, to make a few extra dollars.

This kind of "love" was in it for what could be gained, not what should and could be given. But, somehow, despite everything she had seen, every wound she had nursed, every failure she had been faced with, she was not destroyed. One day, she would learn who to trust. He would guide her to joy in Him, and she would learn to love herself.

Kayla's STORY

Standing outside of the school entrance, leaning against the rough and cold brick wall, Kayla waited anxiously while her phone dialed her mom's number. It rang four times, but there was no answer. Taking a puff on her Marlboro, she let out a sigh. What could her mom possibly be doing? Kayla knew she was probably just at home, so why wasn't she picking up? Glancing at her watch, she saw that she only had five minutes left of her break. So, she called again. Part of her -- the hopeful side -- wanted her mom to pick up, and the other side... almost wished she wouldn't.

"What?" her mom snapped into the telephone.

"Hey, Mom, it's me. I... I have to run, but I wanted to... um, ask you for a small favor..." She really hated doing this, asking her mom for help. Within just a few moments, she felt a throbbing pain at the sides of her forehead -- the beginnings of a headache. It wasn't that she wanted to do everything by herself, but her mom just had a way of making her feel so small, like she was bothering her by simply being alive. So, this call really was her last resort.

Not having heard her mom say anything, she continued.

Her voice growing small and taking on the timid demeanor of a child, despite the fact that she now had her own child, she asked, "Can I ask you to pick up Destiny from the babysitter tonight? I just found out I have another group assignment, and we're probably going to stay late to get started on it."

"No," was all she heard on the other line.

"Why not? I told her I would drop by at 10:30 pm after night school, so you don't have to rush or anything. I just really, really need someone to pick her up, and David's not answering his phone."

"No, because I just don't want to. She's your child. You figure it out."

Taking a deep breath, Kayla responded, "I know she's my child. I never said she was your child. I just…"

Before she could finish her thought, her mom quickly responded, "Ok! So act like you know! I have things to do, and I can't pick her up!"

Looking up into the night sky, Kayla wasn't all that surprised by her mom's response. She had never really been there for her, not when she really needed it, at least.

Drifting off into an old memory, Kayla remembered sitting at home when she was ten. Her mother had just started dating Doug. On this night, in particular, they had made plans to go to a local comedy club, and the babysitter had canceled last minute. "What do you mean you can't come? Where are you now?" her mother demanded.

"How am I supposed to find someone new at the last minute?"

"You know what forget it. Don't bother…" she said, slamming down the phone.

A few minutes later, standing at her room door, her mother looked tired and angry. Leaning on the door frame, she said, "Kay, I'm going out." Looking up from her coloring book and at her mother, Kayla said, "I know. And Betty's not coming. I heard you on the phone."

"Oh. Sorry," she said, making a face, suddenly feeling embarrassed. "I didn't realize I had been that loud. Look, I'll try to be back before you head to bed. Just make sure you don't open the door for anyone. I'll bring my key, and I'm not expecting anyone."

"But what about my English test? Betty was supposed to help me with that."

"Kayla, listen, I don't have time right now. Doug is going to be here any minute now. Just call one of your friends. You guys can work on it together."

Just as she had said, a few moments later, Doug was at the door. And her mom was gone.

So many stories had ended just like that.

After a few moments of unfriendly silence, her mom asked, "Is that all you called for?"

"Yeah. That's all I called for." Disappointed, Kayla added under her breath, "Thanks for nothing."

She hung up and stared out into the empty school parking lot. Besides a few of the night school instructors who drove, the lot was completely vacant. She saw a red Mazda, a silver Audi, and even a BMW X5. Standing in the brisk October air, she let the wind hit her full cheeks and let her mind wander, imagining how much easier life would be if she had a car to get from school, to work, to the babysitter, and grocery store. Just the basic stuff. She didn't need a fancy car either, just something to get her from point A to point B.

Most of the students in the night school program were just like Kayla, finishing up their high school or upgrading credits to apply to college. And, like her, the majority did not have the extra income to be able to afford a car. She flicked her cigarette butt onto the ground, stepped on it, and folded her arms across her narrow frame. By now, her ten-minute smoke break had long been over, but she didn't care. She needed to figure out who was picking up Destiny before she returned to the classroom.

David, her boyfriend, also hadn't been much help lately. She had called him first, as soon as the group assignment was announced, but he hadn't picked up. The last thing she wanted was to go inside and tell her group partners that once again, she wouldn't be able to stay and participate in the assignment breakdown and delegation of tasks. It was clear to her that the other students didn't respect her and thought she was always trying to get out of doing her part. But that wasn't the case. There was just so much going on with her.

Destiny, her five-year-old, was the most beautiful, patient, and easygoing child Kayla could have hoped for. But that didn't change the fact that at the age of 23, Kayla was responsible for not just herself, but another life. Although she lived with her mom, Kayla was beginning to think she would be better off finding an apartment on her own. Simple things like asking her mom to help with Destiny always turned into an argument.

Shifting her attention back to her ringing phone, she listened as the last ring turned into the voicemail message. Again, David hadn't picked up. "Perfect," she concluded sarcastically, her disappointment etched on her face. Letting out a sigh, she said, "There's no one to pick up Destiny. I guess I'll just tell them I can't stay and to just let me know what they decide to go with…" Staring out at the traffic driving by, she thought about starting a second cigarette but decided against it. There was no point in making even more enemies in the class. She was already going to be leaving early. So, she turned, placed her hand on the cold metal door handle, opened the door, and entered the school. For once in her life, Kayla really wished she had one person, just one that she could depend on.

Sometimes, when our desires are so deep, we don't realize that their continued utterance has become a prayer in our minds and on our tongues. We simply know it is a longing of our hearts. As Kayla entered the school, little did she know, her prayer was being heard. God was about to answer. She was going to meet someone who would, in turn, help Kayla meet Kayla. This friend, whose presence was like a light and a mirror, would gently show her that every relationship was a mirror. They reflected back either who she was, or what she had allowed herself to accept. When she began to trust that she could make good decisions for herself, she began expecting so much more of the people around her. When she created a loving and trustworthy relationship with herself, everything changed. Nothing around her had the power to remain the same.

LEARN

Learning is the result of an open heart.

Learning is also the offspring of an open mind.

We don't learn simply because we are in a space where learning is taking place. We must be open to receiving and applying the learning to truly benefit from its presence.

Learning is one of the most precious gifts God gives us during our lifetime.

Imagine if we were born, and the only information we traveled through life with was what our parents decided to speak over us while we were in the womb.

Some of us would have a great advantage over others.

Instead, when we are born, we all have varying capacities to learn. But capacity, nonetheless.

As we pay attention to what is around us, we can add to that database of information we were born with.

Learning is taking place when you are growing.

Learning is evidenced when you are applying.

Learning and healing must travel hand in hand.

Therapy.

She went to therapy for healing. There she learned how much the pain had truly taken root. Therapy, for her, was a grounder. A safe environment to explore what had taken place. To examine the contents of that package that had been destined for her and sent to a child unable to refuse it. But the learning process can be a slow one. The growth was microscopic. But it was still there.

She knew she didn't want to stay wounded. She knew she wanted to be able to trust despite what had happened. She knew she deserved a divinely sourced love; despite the flawed versions she had come to know. But there was such a fight getting there. Getting to a place where she knew and truly believed that she was worthy, not just at the surface but also at a heart, mind, and soul level.

It was a gruesome and violent fight getting to the place where she embraced the truth that what had happened was not the determining story of her life, but rather a line, on a page, in a chapter, in the entire book of her life. She would eventually come to know that her value was found above in the mind and in the uplifting words of a Heavenly Father. In the pages of His book, He had re-written so much joy into the latter end of her story. All she needed to do was keep going.

Keep going.

"What you learn will guide you. Don't ever forget the lessons you have learned. For once you have learned the lesson you can disown the pain" (Evette, 2020).

"The beginning of wisdom is this: Get wisdom. Though it cost all you have, get understanding" (Proverbs 4:7 NIV).

Learn as much as you can about where you have been, about where you are, and about where you want to go.

Your learning speaks to your heart's posture.

For learning is the result of humility. To have learned is the result of having acknowledged that we did not know it all.

There is one who knows all. But He does not share everything He knows with us, because we would not be able to handle the magnitude of it all.

There is such beauty in being able to humble oneself to receive.

Do you know how to receive?

Or are you burdened with the curse of believing you always need to give in order to be worthy?

Daniella

As time progressed, she began to learn new ways of being. She no longer blamed the people around her for the ways they had failed her. She recognized they could not hold her up any more than they were holding themselves up. They could not be any more real with her than they had been with themselves. Nor could they love any deeper than they had loved themselves.

Many had not even begun to scratch the surface of who and what love is. Love is not just an action or a feeling. Love is a person who, through His action, demonstrated to us what love truly is. Because she was open to learning, God Himself was able to become her teacher. He taught her to trust, to learn, and eventually, to feel.

Daniella's STORY

"Come on in," Gabe, her counselor, said with a smile.

Daniella hadn't seen him in months. Taking a look around, she noticed some new art hanging on the walls. His office still had the same smell, however. A combination of Hugo Boss cologne and peppermint because of the variety of plants he insisted on keeping as office décor-one being a thriving peppermint plant. "They help freshen the air and make people smile and feel alive!" Gabe often sang.

As she walked in, Daniella was full of expectation that this time would be productive and would provide some much-needed insight as to why she was feeling so… unlike herself over the past few days. Her sessions with him always helped to give her clarity as to what was really going on with her. Placing her Dior handbag on the couch beside her, Daniella sat down. She chose her favorite spot, the far-right corner of the couch that faced out towards the main street.

Gabe, her counselor, a middle-aged, Bajan man with the most amazingly warm smile, didn't always have the most original things to say, but it was always insightful. Sometimes it wasn't the fact that she hadn't heard someone else say the same exact thing, but somehow, he always had a way of making her feel as if it was the most useful piece of advice she had received on the topic. And, whenever she applied the advice he would provide, there was always a deep learning that would come to rest in her heart and mind and translate into more ease and flow in her life.

"So…," Gabe began, smiling graciously as if he had never seen or heard a sad story in his life, "It's been a while. How have you been?" He asked, tilting his head to the right.

Settling into the couch and making herself comfortable, Daniella responded, "Well, I've been alright. You know, just living my best life!" she added as she chuckled and smiled.

Laughter -- she had just recently discovered -- was one of her favorite ways for deflecting attention away from the seriousness of any given moment. If she could convince the person she was speaking with that the subject was at its core a light-hearted topic and that it didn't really bother her… she didn't have to worry about them thinking she may have been struggling.

"Alright. That's great to hear," Gabe responded, genuinely pleased. Nodding, he added, "So what brings you in today? Were you in the neighborhood? Did you just want to share how great you've been doing?"

He waited and looked intently at his long-time client. It had only been a few minutes since she had entered the office, but he noticed her presence was different -- she was not as guarded. Even her posture and movements had become more fluid, more soft and open.

Knowing him, she knew he wasn't asking to be smart. Gabe was the type of counselor who would be thrilled if a client booked a session simply to let him know how well they were doing. But at his hourly rate, over $9,000.00 an hour, he doubted that was the case in this particular moment. Still, he did not want to assume. So he asked, and waited.

After a few moments of silence, crossing and then un-crossing her legs, Daniella began… "Well, I mean… I definitely am living my best life, but of course… there are a few things that could be better."

Jotting down a few notes, most likely the date, or maybe even the beginnings of a sketch, Gabe looked up. "Alright, well, let's start there. What areas of your life could be better? Start with the first one that comes to mind."

"Well, my relationships -- romantic relationships, to be specific -- are on life support. I meet all these men, but none of them are right! Either they're very accomplished, rich, successful, but their personalities simply will not do, or they're emotionally unavailable, or they're liars…" She drifted off into her own thoughts as she thought about the one man she truly wished was emotionally available.

Gabe sat as she described the men she was meeting, trying his hardest not to smile. He had a feeling this session was going to be about relationships, eventually… but this was right off the bat. This upfront start was an improvement. He noted this thought on his pad of paper.

"…and THAT is why my romantic relationship status is what it is and will remain as is until I meet someone mature enough to tell the truth, be transparent about where he is, and be consistent enough to follow through with the things he says he wants."

Agreeing, Gabe said, "Those are all reasonable traits to expect." After a few moments of silence, he asked, "And what do you think is currently stopping you from meeting this type of man?"

Sighing, Daniella looked out the window. She noticed an elderly woman in a plaid hat, jacket, and gloves walking slowly towards the stoplight. She looked accomplished, settled even. Daniella wondered to herself what that woman's story and life must have been like. She looked as if she didn't have a care in the world…

Turning her head slowly away from the window, she met Gabe's gaze. "I'm not sure, actually."

"Well, let's start with where you meet these men."

"Um, well, some I've met through friends, at events, through working groups that I'm a part of… I've connected with a few on dating apps." Unimpressed by the list she was rattling off, she stopped.

"In essence, I meet men everywhere." Throwing up her hands, she added, "I'll probably meet one right after I leave and am walking to my car!"

Her seemingly dramatic exacerbation made Gabe smile. She had a problem many women would gladly trade places with her to have. "Alright, so that's a good start. You're meeting quite a few men, and all in different contexts and situations."

Stretching his arms above his head, Gabe relaxed his shoulders and put down his notepad. "And what's your thought process towards dating right now? Are you excited to be dating; are you nervous, indifferent? How are you feeling?"

"I mean, I don't really think about dating, to be honest. With work, and my position with the Board of Admissions at the college and traveling for conferences, there's just always something to keep me busy." She reflected a bit more before adding, "I guess the only time I really think about dating is when I go on Facebook or Twitter or something and see posts that remind me I'm 38 and single and not where I want to be in terms of an intimate relationship. Of course, I am working towards it, but it's still not here."

"You know I just feel so alone. I have all these accomplishments, and people always see me as this highly successful woman… and I am," she added, sitting up in her chair. "Everything they see and say about me is true. I just want the same celebration that exists about my public life to be possible for my private life, as well. You know? There's just a disconnect between the two. And it gets really tiring mentally… knowing that my life just isn't what I want it to be in front and behind the scenes. It's easy to put all my thoughts in a box and store them away while I'm working. But eventually the day is over. The meetings are adjourned, and I'm faced with the reality that besides my grandma and my dog, I'm by myself."

Gabe nodded.

"You know…," he began, "it's alright to not feel perfectly aligned in terms of the successes you experience in every area of your life. It's very common to experience great success in one area, even while you are building up another area. Or maybe even as you're aware of the fact that multiple other areas must be built up as well."

"That's true, and I get that. I just want to know what to do about the NOW. The in-between seasons feeling. Because it honestly feels like a weight. I feel it in my chest. It's a -a …tightness, and it's a burden I wish I didn't have to carry."

Daniella had been the first in her family, both on her mother and father's side, to have attended post-secondary, graduated, and then pursued a master's and a doctorate in Chemical Engineering. She knew and recognized there were specific generational patterns she had been called and chosen to break. She was certainly grateful that her life had turned out the way it had. But she would never for a moment deny the empty feeling she sometimes got when she faced herself in the mirror, knowing she had achieved greatness in every area, except for the one that -- for her -- had always mattered the most -- her personal relationships.

Sometimes, late at night, when all the work was completed, all the texts, calls, and meetings had been wrapped up, she would feel the burden of her calling descend on her like an iron blanket. As opposed to the normal use of a blanket to keep you warm and provide a feeling of comfort and safety, this blanket would cause her to feel suffocated and unable to move, breathe comfortably, or even see past that very moment. It was as if the entire responsibility to heal herself, as well as past and future generations, was all calling out to her at once, needing her attention and wondering when she was going to be available to be relied upon.

She thought about her students and how much they praised and looked up to her. Her family members, in particular her nieces, and how they loved when she would come around. Even the young women who constantly reached out to her after a conference or talk to tell her how much her success had inspired them. Daniella was always surprised when they would finish with, "I want to be like you when I grow up." But every so often, if she was honest with herself, she recognized she didn't yet have the capacity to be relied on -- even for herself. And it wasn't that she hadn't come a very long way because she had.

Daniella had forgiven her parents, each for their own sins. Her mother for choosing herself over motherhood. And her father for not choosing her mother. She was born into a dysfunctional story of doubt, pride, selfishness, and personal fear. A story that had been unfolding with broken patterns being repeated in every generation for years before she was ever even a thought. So, when she came into the world, it was no surprise that the welcome she received was not suitable for a new life and vision to be supported and birthed in this world.

She often wondered why the love she had always wanted from her biological parents had always seemed so unattainable. She knew her mother and father, but she had never lived with them for more than a few months. By the time she was two years old, she had already been sent to live with her grandmother on her mother's side. Later on, she had learned all her mother had said to her grandmother was that she couldn't be slowed down by a baby and needed someone to watch her so she could pursue her career. She had dropped her off for what should have been a weekend stay and literally never came back.

She had been the unwanted child.

If it hadn't been for the two Gs, God and Grandma, Big Mama, as everyone called her, Daniella didn't know where her life would have been. Big Mama had shown her unconditional love from the moment she arrived at her home. Although she was already in her 50s and now parenting a young child, she never made Daniella feel as though she was a bother. Far from it. She would go out of her way to let her grandbaby know she was there for her.

One year, when Daniella was about ten years old, she really needed a new winter jacket and pair of warm boots. Big Mama took extra shifts for three weeks, practically begging her co-workers to let her take their shifts, and when even that wasn't enough, she went down to Mr. Bertman's jewelry shop in Midtown and sold one of her favorite necklaces to be able to make sure her grandbaby would be alright. She never complained about the sacrifices she made, and she never said a word to her granddaughter. She figured it was better not to let her "right hand know what her left hand was doing." Besides, if she cared for herself in any dynamic and deep way, she knew she couldn't allow her own offspring to be uncared for in this world.

Big Mama had learned that in order to say she truly valued herself, she must first take care of herself and love on herself. Then from there, every other person and space around her would be supported from the stability and sacred life she had created inwardly. It was in this environment that Daniella had been raised.

In hindsight, it had been a blessing that she had been raised by her mother's mother and not her mother. Her mother just did not have what it would have taken to raise Daniella in a supportive and stable environment. She was barely stable herself.

"You know, Daniella," came Gabe's gentle voice nudging her back to the present moment, "giving yourself permission to not be everyone's hero will not mean their demise."

Furrowing her brow and expressing her confusion by her facial expression, she wondered what that had to do with her dating life, but instead replied, "Go on."

"You may feel as if it is your job to save yourself, support your community, heal the past generational traumas, and set up the future generations for success. While all of that is noble and good, you first need to choose and save yourself."

"It sounds to me that your dissatisfaction in your dating life has nothing to do with the men at all. But more so a discontentment you feel about the unsettled parts of your journey and the weights that you have taken on as your responsibility."

"No man -- and I'm telling you this as a man who has done and continues to do the inner healing work -- will be able to meet every one of your needs. But, if you're open to sitting with yourself, re-learning and re-acquainting yourself with the pieces that haven't been given a voice for years, your entire outlook on what your "responsibility" is to your past and future will evolve. In its evolution, you will find you knew everything you ever needed to know. It truly is an inner knowing."

"It will be a new process for you because you're so used to being in control. You're used to knowing how the story will end, but there are still some paths you have never crossed before, and you will need to rely on God to navigate. It may be a steep learning curve, but as you trust God, you will find He is the best teacher."

FEEL

Feel the pain, but don't stop there.

Pain will be found along the journey, but if you stop at the pain, you will never reach your intended destination.

Feel the pain, but don't worship it.

Do not become so acquainted with it that you hold on to the pain when you have the choice to let it go. Letting it go will create room for healing and restoration.

Imagine how much lighter you will feel once you have let the pain go. Once you stop conversing with that spirit, trying to get to know its name.

Sometimes in trying to avoid feeling the real emotion, we numb ourselves.

We distract ourselves. We do everything but feel.

But the true healing only comes from having been able to conclude something is wrong. I need to get help. I need to apply some treatment.

We shy away from feeling the depth of our pain, but that only prolongs its impact.

The longer we pretend there isn't a problem. The longer the problem is able to continue getting worse.

To feel is one of the bravest things we can do.

To stop and admit that we feel is one of the most powerful ways to take back our control.

Once we know what we feel, then we can decide if this what we want to continue feeling

If not, the good news is there are so many other emotions you can choose from.

Choose to feel. It all.

Beth

She had come to love the idea of being a victim. She loved the attention it would get her. She adored the peoples' comments. How they would vilify her perpetrator and deify her strength. She didn't really want to let go of the pain. After a while, bitterness and anger became part of her makeup. Like a river constantly running over a rock and through a field, their presence becomes embedded in the landscape and leaves a clear crevasse that makes it far easier for more of its kind to follow after it. But just because something has been all you've known does not mean you should continue to welcome it.

"Come to me, all you who are weary and burdened, and I will give you rest. Take my yoke upon you and learn from me, for I am gentle and humble in heart, and you will find rest for your souls. For my yoke is easy and my burden is light" (Matthew 11:28-30 NIV).

Love yourself enough to give yourself the permission to re-welcome joy. There was once a time when joy was common to you. You laughed. You smiled. You were playful. You ran. There was no reason. It was simply who you were. Joy personified. But, as time wore on and life experiences became more vast, you saw more and more reason to refrain from dancing, to avoid smiling at all costs, never wanting to invite additional attention. You began to love the idea of blocking people out with a frown. You were more interested in feeling the anger, rejection, and hurt you had experienced and then internalized. But there is so much more waiting for you.

Beth's STORY

"Owww! Beth gritted her teeth, clenching her jaw from the pain. She stumbled forward as she tried to brace herself from falling, using her left hand to grip the exercise bar in front of her. She wasn't one to complain, even when things hurt deeply, but this was excruciating pain. The type of pain that traveled from the area in question and reverberated loudly through one's entire body. She felt a shiver travel from her neck down her spine, similar to the feeling of a hot drink trickling down your throat -- you feel every movement of the drink, but this was the complete opposite. It wasn't warm and welcomed. It was a cold and sharp shooting pain.

Ever since that night in the accident, she had been experiencing pain all throughout her back and legs, but especially on the right side of her neck. Every time she felt the pain, she would remember why she was lying in a bed or trying to pull herself across the floor, barely able to move. And it was all because of him. They, Beth and Kyle, had been at the same party and had both decided to leave around the same time. Being the responsible person she always was, Beth planned ahead of time to travel by Uber because she knew she would have a few drinks that evening.

It was a Sunday night, and both Kyle and Beth had been invited to their friends' housewarming party. It had actually been a pretty large gathering for an event of that nature. But good old Laney and Jermaine were never known to do things small. They had invited over two hundred people to celebrate the purchase of their latest property, Manor Del Reis. They wanted to christen the home with an eventful night. And that they certainly did.

As with all their other events, there was live entertainment. On this night in particular, depending on the type of music one enjoyed, you could travel from one suite in the home to the next and feel like you were in Mexico, one moment, with men in traditional Sombrero hats and crisp charro outfits playing mariachi music. Their laughter, song, and joy created a warmth that blended so well with the melodies coming from their vihuelas and guitarróns. "México Lindo y querido!" And taking a journey just a few steps away, entering into a private soundproof auditorium, you would feel like you had entered a completely different environment. This time, a 90s house party in uptown Harlem with a DJ spinning what was once the latest in Hip-Hop and R&B.

Jermaine had invited a chef, one of his good friends, Louis, to "have fun," creating a menu for the night. The smell of braised lamb chops and au jus, sautéed vegetable appetizers, and mango puree wafted through the air. What was even more impressive is that they hadn't even begun to bring out the desserts yet! Everywhere you looked, people were enjoying themselves; laugher and camaraderie were the themes of the night. Good food and great company were abundant. The alcohol unlimited. Laney and Jermaine, greeting all their friends and family, felt an overflow of joy and gratitude that everyone had come out to support and celebrate this milestone with them. This wasn't their first home, but after a year like they had just had, every moment with loved ones felt that much more precious.

Beth, keeping in mind she had an important meeting the next day, decided to head out just slightly before 11:45 pm. And having noticed when she first arrived that the walk from the gate to the front entrance of the home was a long one, she said goodbye to Laney, one of her best friends from middle school, and Jermaine, the only man who had ever been able to get and hold Laney's attention. After their goodbye hugs and kisses, as well as promises to catch up soon, she left their home and closed the solid, hand-carved oak door behind her. That door is so Lane! she thought to herself.

Humming as she walked along the newly paved driveway, Beth was so thankful she had thrown her flats in her bag. Manor Del Reis was a beautiful property overlooking Mavis Beach. It sat statuesquely at the top of a hill. As she walked down the driveway, she chuckled to herself as she concluded her heels were cute but definitely would not have done the job.

Stopping to find her cellphone in her Coach clutch, she pulled it out, opened the flashlight app on her phone, thinking to herself, Man, I know they just bought this house, but they really need to get some lights out here! I can't see a thing. Not wanting to walk directly down the middle of the driveway, she moved off to the right side, trying her best not to stumble over any of the rocks that were lining the path. Inhaling a deep breath of the cold night air, she understood why Laney had always loved the outdoors. It was almost as if the air here was filtered. Unadulterated, pure. Not just that, but it was so calm and peaceful. She pulled on her jacket strings and drew her coat closer to her waist.

Back at the party, Jermaine's friend, Kyle, had also just decided he was going to head out. Having walked around to a few locations - pool, theatre room, main floor dining, and even the second-floor art gallery - and not having seen Laney or Jermaine, he decided to just head out and text them the next day. He descended the grand staircase and made his way across the main entrance to the east wing visitor coat closet. Scanning through all the black coats, he quickly recognized his jacket. It was a burgundy trench coat he had picked up on his last trip to Italy. As he pulled it out, his wallet fell. Reaching down, he stumbled forward but braced himself against the wall.

"You ok there?" came a woman's voice from behind him. Turning around, he felt the room spin and struggled to focus on the very short, very cute, Asian woman standing in front of him.

"Oh yeah. I'm good," he responded, "I just dropped something. That's all."

"Oh, alright," she said, looking directly at him as she tried to see if his eyes were red or if he was slurring his words. Neither was the case. Raising her eyebrows, she added, "Ok, well, I'm sure Laney and

Jermaine wouldn't mind if you stayed over. You know… in case you needed to sleep or anything."

Raising his hands as if to say, "no need," Kyle shook his head. "No, no. I'm good. I'm only going a couple of minutes up the road." He put on his jacket and patted his pockets to locate his keys. No need to spend the night, he thought to himself dismissively. I only had a couple of Stellas, a few shots of Jameson, and one Old Fashioned, or maybe it had been two? Or was it three? Kyle honestly couldn't remember, but he knew he was fine to drive home.

Stepping outside, he realized with the first gust of fall air that hit him that it had gotten much cooler than he expected. He looked around and located his car, making sure to walk there as quickly as he could. Opening the car door and sitting down, he placed his phone and wallet on the passenger seat beside him. Reaching over, he turned on the heat and connected his Bluetooth. He was greeted by the sound of brass, a defined bass, drums, and Jay-z rapping, "I feel like a Black republican, money I got coming in. Can't turn my back on the hood too much love for them…" Classic Nas, Kyle thought to himself. Nothing would ever take the place of the sound and mood you got from early 2000s music.

Speeding off the lot that had been reserved for visitor cars, Kyle smiled as he thought about how much he enjoyed driving manual. He put the car into first gear and began his descent. Rounding the corner, his phone slid off his leather interior and landed on the floor on the passenger side of his car. Glancing over quickly, he saw that the phone wasn't too far. Keeping his left hand on the wheel, he reached over to grab it with his right. It couldn't have been more than two seconds that he was looking away, but in those couple seconds, his car drifted, and the next thing he knew, he heard a loud thud. He slammed on the breaks and stopped his car. He couldn't see anything, even with his high beams on. Thinking he had hit a raccoon or some other animal, Kyle cautiously opened the driver's side door to his car. He wanted to at least see the damage that had been done.

His car door opens.

He steps outside.

He looks

She lays there.

He curses.

She cries.

He runs his hands through his hair.

She tries to turn her head.

Panicked. He freezes.

Pained. She freezes.

Rounding the corner, down an incline, in those couple seconds he had taken to reach for his phone, Kyle had hit Beth walking towards her Uber. After nine days in a medically induced coma, Beth had awoken to find she could barely breathe without the slightest movement of her chest bringing with it some sort of pain. Her right leg had been broken in two places, and the right side of her rib cage fractured. Her spine required chiropractic adjustments for re-alignment and reduction of pressure from the inflammation the impact had caused.

Beth was feeling the impact of the collision in more ways than she cared to admit. And although she was a believer and knew the Bible said, "Forgive so that you can be forgiven," the last thing she found herself wanting to do was to forgive Kyle. In fact, in the weeks and months that followed, Beth would often find herself repeating the details of that night to anyone who would listen -- her friends, family members, strangers even. In her mind, Kyle had ruined her life.

The meeting she was supposed to have had the next day could have changed her entire career. After years of networking, interning, studying, and consistently elevating her value, she had secured a meeting with one of the top marketing firms in the world. They had been interested in partnering with her company to access her extremely sought-after consultation services. While logically she knew that she could still have another shot, the timing couldn't have been worse. The process of advancing her career to where she finally had gotten it to had been a long and unusually challenging one. When the pain hit her, she often found herself crying not simply because it hurt physically but also because of everything she believed that moment had stolen from her.

So, on this particular morning at physiotherapy, Beth was truly feeling the pain of having to "start all over." Re-learning to stand, to walk, to sit up, all of it. If there was anything she had learned over these past few months, it was that emotional pain was often exacerbated by physical pain. Those months she spent laying in a bed had given her a lot of time to think, and she concluded that there was nothing she wanted, no needed, more than to secure her emotional healing as she also strengthened her physical healing, as well.

As she paused to steady herself from her stumble, she remembered the conversation she had had with her sister the day before. It hadn't ended well. It hadn't ended horribly, either, but it had definitely made Beth think. She wondered whether the things her sister had said about her were true. She hadn't been mean about it, more so concerned.

She heard her sister's soft voice, "Beth, I know it hurts, but you're becoming bitter. Every time I talk to you, you're complaining about what's going wrong and talking about what you can't do. I love you, and that's the only reason I'm telling you this. You can't keep nursing this bitterness and think you're going to get better."

Coming up behind her, Tiffany, one of the physiotherapists noticing Beth's stumble, came to see if she needed any support.

"No. But thanks so much, Tiffany. I'm just more frustrated today than anything. It's not so much the pain as it is… the fact that I'm even here."

"Mmm. Yeah, I hear you," Tiffany said. "You know a lot of the patients who come in here have the same question as you, why. Why them? Why now? So, you're definitely not alone in that sentiment." She gave Beth a sympathetic look.

As if thinking more to herself than anything, she added, furrowing her brow, "One thing that is different about your story, however, is the fact that the guy who hit you came to visit you every day while you were in a coma at the hospital. Now that I've never heard of!"

Looking at Tiffany as if she had just grown a third eye, Beth was as confused as she'd probably ever been. "What do you mean the person who hit me visited me every day?"

"Yeah, every day while you were in a coma, he came and inquired as to how you were doing at the hospital." Noticing the confused and surprised expression on Beth's face, she added, "It's right there in your file. I thought you knew…" she added, her voice drifting off.

Still seeing the same shocked expression on her face, Tiffany concluded Beth knew nothing about it. She decided to give her a moment with the news.

Shifting her weight from one leg to the other, Tiffany concluded, "Well, that's awkward! I thought you knew." Looking down at the envelope she had in her hand, she added, "This piece of mail arrived for you today." She handed it to Beth, asked again if she was ok, and when she assured her she was, she left.

Later on that afternoon when Beth sat down in her room at the rehabilitation center, she decided to open the envelope she had gotten.

Oddly enough, there was no return address. Strange, she thought to herself but decided to open it, nonetheless. It was definitely addressed to her: Bethany Millwood.

Opening the small envelope, she pulled out the card. It read:

Beth,

You don't know me, but my name is Kyle. I'm the person who hit you when you were going home from Jermaine and Laney's. I know there's really nothing I can say that would take back what happened, but I do want you to know I am so sorry. I have been looking for ways to be able to make it up to you, but there really is nothing that could. So, instead of feeling sorry for how pathetic my actions were, I would like to ask if you would allow me to assist you in your recovery process. If that looks like grocery runs or driving you to therapy, I'll do it. I just want you to know you're not alone in feeling this pain. I'm responsible for causing it, so I will definitely be responsible to help you move forward.

Here's my number... and, of course, I understand if you want nothing to do with me, but hopefully, you'll use it.

Kyle

Before she got to the end, Beth began to cry. For the first time since waking up from her coma, she started to picture Kyle as a person and not a monster. Someone who had made a mistake and who was genuinely sorry. Propping herself up on her bed, adjusting one of the pillows under her lower back, she reached over and grabbed a tissue. Her sister was right. She had become bitter. She had chosen to see herself as a victim. But the truth was she was fortunate to even be alive and to not have had any more injuries than she had incurred.

Turning her head and staring out of the window, she studied the trees that were blowing furiously this way and that because of the wind. You know what, she thought to herself, I deserve to feel happy. I deserve to try again, and I'm not going to let the experience of pain rob me of the life I can still have. I'm going to feel every feeling, but I won't give them any more power or meaning than they deserve to have.

Tapping her left hand with the card, Beth looked at the bottom of the note where Kyle had left his number. "I don't think I'm up to it today, but maybe… just maybe I'll give him a call tomorrow."

Sometimes, in our pain, we feel like we are the only ones "feeling" what we are feeling. We tell ourselves the story that the only ones in pain are us, especially when someone else can be pointed to as the cause of our pain. We can wrongfully believe that we are the only ones that are feeling the repercussions of an event.

The truth is, pain is an equal opportunity type of experience. It does not discriminate. What touched Beth in this moment was the ability to see beyond herself. To recognize someone else's pain as not separate from hers, but in addition to hers. She was hurting, and so was Kyle. As you heal, allow yourself to be open to the idea that your pain is not independent of everyone around you but likely part of an interdependent web. A web that you CAN become free from.

GROW

Growth is so beautiful.

To grow in spite of loss, grief, pain, disappointment, anger, violence, rejection, mistreatment, and betrayal is powerful beyond belief.

It is powerful because there were so many other options available, but to choose life and growth says that you still have hope.

Growth cannot be accomplished and sustained outside of intentional choice.

Growing looks like asking for help when you need it.

Growing looks like placing yourself first on your priority list.

Growing looks like prioritizing your goals and your well-being without apology.

Growing looks like self-awareness that does not lead to a complete overhaul of your most precious and genuine self.

Growing looks like being able to handle the character flaws that God points out -- without feeling discouraged and attacked. It's all for your good. Never your harm.

Breah

Her growth took the form of changed friendships and relationships. It also took the form of new interests and hobbies. She wanted a husband and children one day, but she no longer welcomed the presence of a man at the expense of her God. It wasn't an overnight process, but little by little, she started trading time texting them to reading His word. Nothing felt more satisfying. Nothing felt more right than cultivating a strong relationship with the One who had saved her so many times over. Her growth was not recognized by everyone, mind you. But it was taking place.

Some of the closest people to her didn't realize that she was growing. She was growing so beautifully. They couldn't see because they were blinded by who she used to be. They were blinded by the memories of what she used to do, the things she used to say, and the experiences she used to have. But if they would only stop and really sit with the idea of her, they would see she had grown immensely.

The enemy had tried to completely destroy her, reduce her to a shell she could not come out of. Block her from speaking, from sharing, from opening her mouth, and from telling her story. If she ever learned who she was, if she ever believed what God said about her, if she ever gained the confidence that comes from hearing the voice of God whisper, "You are beautiful, you are enough, you are safe and loved," nothing would ever be the same. The enemy had been close. This plan had almost been accomplished, but right when everything would have reached the tipping point, He sent help. This would be the start of her growth journey. Never looking back, she would become the most powerful version of herself. Someone she never even imagined she could become.

Breah's STORY

Walking into the kitchen where her mom was washing dishes, Breah stood at the entrance and leaned against the now off-white wall. "Mom, I have to talk to you about something."

After a long day of work, and having come home to a messy apartment, dishes in the sink, and nothing put away from the grocery trip the day before, the only thing Michelle wanted to hear her daughter say was, "Don't worry Mom, I'll take care of dinner tonight. You've done enough work today."

Instead of that, she heard her daughter say, "I'm pregnant."

Silence.

Heavy and weighted quietness.

If you could be killed by the weight of heaviness, the silence that followed Breah's statement would have taken you out. Her mother, a 36-year-old single mother, stopped what she was doing. She stopped scrubbing the soapy plate in her hand, rested it down in the sink, and turned to look at her daughter. Leaning on the counter and crossing her arms across her chest, she looked as if she had aged ten years in just a few seconds.

"You're pregnant," she repeated, not a question, just a confirmation to herself mostly of what her daughter had just said.

Shifting her weight from one leg to the other, Breah said, "Yes. I'm ten weeks."

"Ten weeks?! You've got to be kidding me! Have you even been to the doctor yet?" Michelle wasn't sure exactly what she looked like, but she was certain the facial expression she was wearing was one of horror, anger, and shock. She could feel her temperature rising and remembered from her sessions at group therapy that she was nearing her breaking point of rage. She reminded herself to breathe, one, two, three, four seconds in… one, two, three, four seconds release. Shaking her head, she ran her hand through her thick brown curls. There weren't very many moments she could remember when she genuinely had nothing to say, but this was just one of those moments.

Pulling out a chair at the dining room table, Breah sat down and let out a sigh. She hadn't known exactly what to expect, but this conversation was already not taking the best of turns. Her usually loud, happy, talkative mother had suddenly become quiet. "Yeah, I have. I went as soon as I found out. I called dad, too."

Suddenly snapping out of the daze the news of her daughter's pregnancy had drawn her into, she turned her head as if in slow motion and asked with an incredulous expression, "Wait, you spoke to your father? You told him… before you told me!?"

Suddenly, they were no longer having a conversation about the fact that Breah was pregnant. The news that Breah had spoken to her father and had told him about the pregnancy before her mom became much more important of a topic. Immediately sensing the hurt in her mom's voice, Breah tried to get in front of the emotional tsunami she knew would follow. She hadn't wanted to hurt her mom. That was definitely the last thing she had wanted, so she immediately tried to explain.

"Well, yeah, he owns a whole bunch of medical centers, and we don't have insurance. I got a test from the drug store. Well, a couple of them, and when they all came back positive, I knew we wouldn't have the money to pay for the appointments, so I called him."

Picking at her nails, she added, "I actually found his number online. I searched his name on Google and typed in Phoenix. That's all I knew, but his centers were right there up at the top. It said Michael

Alterman Medical, so I called. This lady picked up, and I asked if Michael was there. You know… dad never told anyone there about me. Maybe not even at all."

Growing concerned about where this story was heading, Michelle looked at her daughter and asked for clarification. "What do you mean? How do you know that?"

"I heard her. She probably thought she had put me on mute, but I heard the whole conversation. She asked people, I don't know who, just someone there, 'Does Mr. Alterman have kids? There's a girl on the line asking for Michael, and she says he's her dad.'"

Michelle, who had since joined Breah in sitting at the table, placed her hand on top of her daughter's. "Honey, I'm so sorry."

"It's ok, Mom. It's not your fault." She reflected for a moment and added, "It's no one's fault."

At the age of 17, Breah had always been extremely reflective and mature and was demonstrating this maturity yet again. She always had a beautiful ability to see situations from almost any angle, no matter what part of the story she fell on. Today was no exception. Shaking her head in amazement at how her daughter had been holding in this information and was now relaying it so calmly, Michelle asked, "So what did he say?"

Using her finger to trace the design of the placemat in front of her, Breah began, "Well first…" she said, sounding annoyed, "… he didn't even know who I was. I said my name like three times! And, finally, when I said I'm your daughter, he finally got it."

Sitting in silence, they both had been consumed with their own thoughts about the ghost that was Michael Alterman. For one, he was the symbol of a failed relationship that, for once, had produced something good. For the other, he was the symbol of what type of parental relationship not to re-create. What was supposed to be a moment of transparency about her pregnancy had turned into a conversation about her dad. Having noticed the pattern of how he always seemed to become the focus and seeing how it always made her mom sad, Breah decided to finish off the story.

Releasing the sigh she didn't realize she had been holding onto, she continued, "So, yeah, I told him I might be pregnant, and I asked if he could help me get a doctor." Allowing her daughter to tell her own story, Michelle waited and gave her daughter the fullness of her attention.

"He didn't ask me anything. He just said he knew a good doctor here in Tennessee, a pregnancy one, who would take care of me. He got me the number and told me to call them in two days after he had gotten a chance to talk to her."

"So, she's my doctor now. I guess dad is paying for it. I'm not sure. But I've gone to see her twice - once to meet her and once for an appointment. I like her. She's nice."

Almost no louder than a whisper, she added, "Maybe next time you can come with me." Finally, looking up from the dining room table at her mom, she noticed she had been crying. Freezing with surprise, Breah didn't really know what to make of the sight. She had never seen her mom cry before.

"Of course, I'll come, baby. I'm not going to lie. I am not happy you're having a baby at this age, at least. It's hard," was all she added as a single tear rolled down her cheek. "But I would never leave you, Bree. I may not always love what you do, but my heart will always be for you. I will never stop loving you."

The clock on the wall said 7:48 pm. They had only been speaking for thirty minutes, but if you had told either one of them that they had been there for two hours, they probably would have believed you.

Getting serious again, Michelle's facial expression changed as she again folded her arms across her chest. She said, "Now, what I really want to know is who the father is."

Cheering and applause broke Breah's train of thought. Startled, she looked around and remembered where she was, realizing she had been replaying a seventeen-year-old memory of telling her mom she was pregnant with Miguel. However, in this present moment, seventeen years had passed, and here she was sitting at his high school graduation.

Looking up at all the graduates in their gowns, she scanned with her eyes to locate Miguel. He was smiling and looking down, probably texting Josue, his best friend, sitting two seats away. Taking a deep breath and looking over to her mom sitting on her right, she felt so much happiness welling up in her heart. Never in her wildest dreams would she have imagined that moment of transparency would have been the start of a brand-new era in their relationship. It was that day that they began living with a newfound transparency and honesty. They had spoken about so much that day and agreed to never hold secrets from one another.

When Miguel was born, he was invited into that very same space of understanding. That one conversation had supported the growth of a beautiful and strong family unity, and Breah never forgot her mother's promise. "I may not always love what you do, but my heart will always be for you. I will never stop loving you." Looking from her mom over to her left, she noticed even her dad seemed to be moved by the significance of the moment. The three of them had never actually attended any event together before. But not surprisingly, Miguel, whose name meant "Who is like God?" had brought them all together. Reaching over and taking her mom's hand in hers, she squeezed it and thanked God quietly in her heart for the growth that He had foreseen and had blessed her by allowing her to also see and feel in this moment. The graduates were standing now and preparing to be called to receive their diplomas. The graduation program listed them all alphabetically. As she saw her son's name, "Miguel Alterman," she smiled as she realized the one whose name reminded her there was no one like God was also the one who had helped her to see there was also no one who could restore her joy like Him either.

EXAMINE

One of the most undeniable gifts of pain is the opportunity to reflect.

An invitation to examine ourselves.

Some of the most life-changing moments and revelations will come from simply being honest and real enough with ourselves to answer the questions we probably should have been asking before the pain.

What was God trying to say all along?

What themes were made clear when the pain stopped you in your tracks?

Where do you want to go next?

Who and what will be chosen and found worthy to continue on?

What does 'after this' look like?

What needs to change in order to make the new desired reality a possibility?

Is there anything that needs to stay the same? Or perhaps evolve?

Chelsea

It took years for her to begin to ask herself these questions. She hadn't been ready until God stopped everything and gave her nothing to focus on but herself. She couldn't hide behind work and volunteering and mentorship roles. None of it was usable anymore as an excuse not to look at herself. It was painful. And it was scary, but every day she showed up to face herself.

Unknown to her would be how long this would continue, but what she did know was that this was where she needed to be. This place of self-examination and silence felt right. Prior to that, not much had "felt right" for a very long time. But because she had been brave enough to honestly look at herself, she began to see what truly needed healing. And, God, the proud Father that He always is, began to assist in the process. Anything for His baby girl. Anything to help her heal.

He would send people to encourage her, people to pray with and for her, songs and sermons that uncovered the demons that needed to be dealt with. He sent it all. Most importantly, He sent His word—Rhema words, ones that were specific to the exact time and situation. Always perfect for what was being felt in that moment. Every one of those words was perfectly timed. They helped her know what her Heavenly Father was saying while she was also making her own declarations. It was important to self-examine, but it was, and will always be, more important to hear what Abba (God) is saying about your conclusions.

Chelsea's STORY

It was 2 pm on a Thursday afternoon. Chelsea and her younger sister, Arielle, stopped at the bank before picking up some items Chelsea had ordered for her clothing line. As they walked into the branch, every teller was occupied with another customer. They joined the line. Although she could see the faces of the tellers working that day, she could only see the backs of the individuals being serviced. Waiting, they scrolled on their cellphones and made small talk, pointing out funny memes on Instagram to each other. As one customer left, they moved closer to the front of the line.

Not having paid much attention to those around her, Chelsea was a bit surprised to look up from her phone when she heard someone say, "Chelsea?" Immediately, she recognized Marcus. He had been the customer being helped right in front of them and had just finished being served when he turned around to see her. Although it had been years since they had seen each other, he hadn't changed much since the fifth grade. Still the same smile. Still the same babyface.

"Marcus! How are you? I haven't seen you in such a long time." Chelsea and her family had lived in the same area all her life. She had attended elementary, middle, and part of high school with Marcus. A few years ago, while running some errands, she had seen him but hadn't heard of or connected with him since.

They greeted each other with a hug, and he responded, "I'm doing well. How are you?"

"I'm great," she said with a smile, genuinely happy to see him. "What have you been up to?"

They made small talk and decided to exchange numbers and contact information, both agreeing that they should meet up in the near future. As he left, they gave one another one last hug, and he said to her, "You look amazing."

A few years before this encounter, Chelsea had been sitting with God. She was having a moment of reflection and was unpacking some of the baggage that had accumulated over the years. In this particular moment, she was dealing with the belief that told her she wasn't enough. She knew how to unpack and confront the lie.

First, she had to acknowledge the fact that she had been believing one. Next she had to really identify why she believed it and where it had come from.When she started listing out the moments that led her to believe she was not enough, one of the first moments that came to her mind was a day in fifth grade. On this particular day, sitting in her homeroom classroom, a pink portable being used by the school because they had run out of classroom space inside, she placed her head down on her desk and started crying -- hot tears running down her little brown face. She didn't know where the teacher had been at the time, but no one noticed her crying or came over to ask what was wrong.

The two boys who sat directly in front of her had been making fun of her for being skinny. Marcus, one of the two boys, was a popular kid. So was Chelsea, but that didn't stop the other kids from letting her know just how "skinny" she was at what seemed like every chance they got. She had heard it so often before, but that didn't stop the words from hurting her on this particular day. No, she felt all of it. So, over twelve years later, when at the age of 26, she had allowed God to begin dealing with all of her insecurities, this moment immediately entered into her consciousness as a moment she needed to unpack and resolve.

She was enough regardless of what anyone had said, any experiences that told her she wasn't, or any moments that had begun to assert themselves as truth. She was enough, not because she had "grown into her looks" or had become more beautiful. No, she was enough because God had made her that way. It wasn't the compliments and the attention she had received over the years that had changed her mind and opened her eyes to her value; it was the word and affirmation of her Heavenly Father.

The healing that God had brought through her willingness to open up had mended the soul wounds that, if left uncared for, would have festered and been passed down. So, on this Thursday afternoon, she smiled, and a deep joy sprang up in her heart when she recognized God brought the very person who had contributed to one of her deepest wounds to come back and tell her something she no longer needed anyone to tell her. She already knew she was enough. God had been trying to tell her all along. Finally, she believed it.

EVOLVE

To evolve is to affirm, I want more.

To evolve is to admit, I acknowledge more is available to me, and I believe I am worthy of it.

To evolve is to decide I am not afraid of leaving behind what I know, for what I don't yet know.

Evolution will cost you what you have been and what you have known.

If you can admit there are greater heights to be reached, and give yourself permission to evolve, what you leave behind will always be worth it in favor of your peace and progress.

To evolve is to boldly declare, I am going forward whether anyone comes with me or not.

Mia

There was a time all the pieces of her life seemed so misplaced and so misaligned that even she could not imagine that things could change. Or that it would be possible for them to be different. She had grown up with parents who spoke to her about Christ and God, but she didn't know what a personal relationship with her Heavenly Father was like. She didn't have one.

There had been moments of darkness and loss, extreme pain, and some of it she brought on herself, but other moments were not her choosing or her orchestration. Looking at all the pieces one day, she said to herself, "You know what? I want more than this. I don't want this pain anymore. I don't want this feeling of inadequacy and regret. I want all that God originally intended for me to have." And so, she began to ask God, "Change how I think. The things I look at may not change, but my perspective certainly can. The immediate situation may not be positively impacted if I decide right now to change my mind, but, eventually, I know it can have a positive impact."

She began her process of evolving. It started first with how she spent her time. She would spend hours just getting to know God and allowing Him to tell her who she was outside of the abortions, outside of the abusive relationship, outside of the brokenness, outside of it all. And He spoke such kind words to His daughter. They would dance and laugh, and she would cry as she listened to Him tell her how much He loved her. She began to know that even in those dark moments, He had been there. And He was so proud of her for choosing to befriend joy. It was one of His most precious gifts. He wished more people would receive it! Not only that, but He blessed her with peace because she had chosen to be the woman who believed no matter how dark things had gotten, the light was still her portion.

Mia's STORY

Clearing his throat and glancing at his notes for the upcoming interview, Dave looked at the radio show technician who was counting him in. Holding up three fingers, then two, then one, the technician motioned, and then Dave saw the all too familiar flashing and lit sign "ON AIR." It was showtime.

"Welcome everyone to today's episode of Impact: I Said What I Said, where we interview men and women who are at the top of their game, leading their industries and businesses at the highest level. I hope you've had an amazing weekend, but even if you haven't, today's show is about to get your week started off right! And that, my friends, is a personal guarantee I am making to you!"

The intro music began to play, and Dave smiled, excited to get into the interview with a woman whose brand, business, and impact he had been following for over ten years. Her work had personally touched his life, and he could barely wait to tell her once off the air.

"Today, we have an outstanding show lined up for you with a guest who I am so excited to be speaking with! Mrs. Mia Tulloch has been coaching individuals in the area of personal development for over a decade. She is the founder of the coaching program 'Upgrade your Stinking Thinking' that has impacted millions of individuals and families in the journey of becoming all that God desires for them to be. She has been featured on various national television programs, podcasts, online conferences, and events. Her latest book, Charge Your Worth and Do Not Give Discounts! has quickly become a New York Times bestseller, with people stating this is the most real account they have found of what the process of 'becoming' truly costs and how it deserves to be viewed and respected. Please help me welcome Mrs. Mia Tulloch to the show!"

There was a pause as the show technicians played a backing track of audience applause.

"Mrs. Tulloch, thank you so much for being here today."

Sitting back in the studio chair, Mia adjusted her Tom Ford glasses. "Thank you so much for having me. It's truly my pleasure, and I'm looking forward to this conversation! And please, just call me Mia."

Reflecting to herself about the magnitude of this moment, Mia couldn't help but smile and thank God for how good He had been. Just as the host had mentioned, her latest book had only been out for three months but had already garnered attention from heavyweights in the self-development field and industry. What started out as the journey of one broken and lost young girl had turned into the story of a successful, determined, and blessed businesswoman, wife, and mother taking the world by storm and remembering to thank Jesus publicly at every chance she got. She honestly would never have imagined her life would be as it was, especially because of where she started.

"So…" Dave began as he reached out and adjusted the height of the mic in front of him. "For the benefit of those listening at home, I want you to know that we -- my team and I -- have been hoping to get Mrs. Tulloch," he paused, "… I mean Mia on this show for ages! But every time we reached out to her, she was booked! Or traveling or just unable to make it. But, finally, we were able to get this time booked! And, boy, do I feel blessed!"

Laughing to himself mostly, Dave turned to Mia, "How are you doing today?"

"I'm doing amazing. I'm so grateful for what God is doing in my life."

"I can only imagine! I recently purchased a copy of Charge Your Worth and Do Not Give Discounts! and when I went the first time, there were quite a few copies at the store, but the next day when I stopped by to pick up a copy for my mother, there were none left at the very same store! Tell me what these past few months have been like for you with the launch of this book."

"Well, they've certainly been a whirlwind! I had a feeling the book was going to be a hit. I truly don't ever pursue any projects unless I believe God has given me the go-ahead, so with that understanding, I honestly believed it was the right time to launch this book and address this topic, but I could never in my wildest dreams have envisioned the success – and right out of the gate – that this book has created!" Turning to face Dave, she added, "It's been massive momentum! My team has been working around the clock to keep the books on the shelves!"

Chuckling to himself, Dave glanced at his next set of questions. "Oh, I know! What do you think is causing this book to resonate so deeply with audiences all around the world?"

Mia thought for a moment, noticing for the first time since she arrived that a crowd of people, likely the radio station employees, had gathered just outside the plexiglass mirror and seemed to be listening in on the interview. The thought that people would stop to come and hear what she had to say brought so much joy to her heart.

"Well, I think the conversations we've been having in the space of self-development have been great, very forward-thinking, and cutting edge. However, as I would speak to clients, one thing I noticed was that there were commonalities amongst the stories and struggles they were sharing."

Nodding and encouraging her on, Dave waited for her to continue.

"Number one, no one was really talking about the sacrifices you'd have to make in the area of relationships. So, when people would encounter resistance in this area, they started to automatically assume they were doing something wrong and needed to tweak their success plan, if you will."

"I hear you. That's always a touchy subject and a difficult area to navigate."

"It is! It certainly is. Now I am not saying that you need to cut off all your friends and family to succeed! Absolutely not. You will need a solid support system in place that will probably be comprised of exactly that, friends and family. But what I am saying is that there will likely be some people you will need to leave behind. Not because they aren't good people, but by virtue of walking different paths, eventually you will look around, and they will no longer be standing beside you."

Taking a sip of his coffee, double cream, double sugar, Dave asked, "And is that something you experienced personally? Because you do go quite in depth in your book about relationships and being willing to make a decision for your success, regardless of who comes with you."

Nodding her head in complete agreement, Mia said, "I did experience that, yes."

"And how did you navigate that process? What helped you stick to your resolution for your success?"

"A few things, actually. I remembered where I had been. The stress that I experienced at the height of my financial struggles, not being able to feed my family, and recognizing that there were people who I knew who were chilling financially, completely stable and secure!"

Mia thought about one moment in particular when all she had left in her fridge were two eggs. There were no other groceries in the entire apartment. Hoping to cook them later on, she remembered how devastated she had been when she walked into the kitchen only to see that her three-year-old son had somehow opened the fridge, taken out the eggs, and dropped both of them on the ground. That moment etched in her mind, she remembered it like it was yesterday. She had fallen to the ground, tears running down her cheeks, sobbing and crumpled on the kitchen floor. Not because the eggs had been dropped but because they represented everything she had left.

"When I hit rock bottom," Mia added, "I knew something had to change. I decided to change myself first before anything else. I decided joy would be my portion in spite of the dark times I had seen and lived through. We had some really tough times as a family! I even knew the debt collection creditors by name!" With a chuckle, she said, "I can laugh about it now, but I would literally recognize which of the agencies was calling and be able to say, 'Hey Lisa, Hey Andrew', or whoever was calling... and I'd tell them I didn't have their money." At the time, of course, it wasn't funny. But it was just a constant barrage of reminders from banks to my empty fridge to collection agencies that my money was reflecting a broken cycle of thought that I had locked myself into.

"So, when I tell people your growth and evolution will cost you everything you've ever known, it is the truth... but it should also come as good news! Some things in life are just not worth keeping and carrying forward into our futures."

"That's good! I'm glad this interview is being recorded because I am certainly going to go back and have a listen and take some notes. Having been in this industry for over a decade, having spoken to thousands of people, what would you like to tell the aspiring solopreneur or entrepreneur about self-development and the evolution they will experience as they grow?"

"Number one, they need to decide what they want. What are your goals for your business? How much do you want to make? What type of lifestyle are you trying to create? Get very, very clear on this. Number two, they need to believe they are worth the more that they desire. Finally, like we mentioned, they have to be willing to go and get it." Pausing for a brief moment, she added, "And willing to go alone. Regardless of whether others understand, support, or decide to join them or not. It has to be a decision they make and hold on to for themselves. That's what I did, and I've never regretted my decision for even a second." Soaking in the truth she had just shared, they both paused and sat for a moment, reflecting on the response.

Nodding his head and really grounding himself in the present, Dave finally responded, "I love that last part you added, about being willing to go alone. That is truly the question I feel many people have not yet answered for themselves. Will I pursue this dream if no one I know supports me? That's truly the determining factor to whether they will persist in the face of resistance. Before we wrap up today, what final thoughts do you have that you would like to share?"

"Final thoughts?" Mia took a deep breath and placed her hand under her chin. "Hmm… I would say, trust God. What I mean by that, in a practical sense, is that when you are in the process of building your dream life, you will find that many doors seem to be closed to you. But the real test is not whether you see the closed door and decide to knock or simply walk away, but knowing which door is worth your time in pursuing, although currently closed. I can't tell you how many times something seemed impossible, but because I trusted God and got His insight, I knew without a shadow of a doubt that this door was one I was supposed to keep knocking at. So, place your confidence in Him to show you which door is one to walk away from…" with a smile, she finished her thought, "…and, of course, which ones to bring out the battering ram to open."

"Well, ladies and gentlemen, you can't see me, but I am grinning from ear to ear. Mrs. Tulloch…," correcting himself, he said, "Mia…

I cannot thank you enough for your presence here with us today. We are so extremely grateful that you have made the time to be on this show. Please let our listeners know how they can connect with you."

Drifting off into her own thoughts, Mia thanked God. Lord, she thought, I never would have made it without You. Thank you for holding my hand through it all. Thank You for helping me to trust You, learn from the failures, helping me be brave enough to feel all the pain, grow through it, reflect, examine my own wounds, and eventually evolve into the woman I am now. Lord, it certainly wasn't easy, but I wouldn't trade my journey for the world. I know now, it was worth it all.

PRAYER

Dear God,

Thank You. Thank You for loving me so deeply that every time I believed a lie about who I was and what I was capable of, You immediately put into action a plan that would destroy the lie. Thank You for Your patience. When I think about the scripture that says Your gentleness has made me great, I recognize this truth in so many areas of my life. You've been so patient with me. Through my process, through my growth. Through my doubt. Through it all. I'm still growing, and I'm still learning to trust. But thank You so much for having extended Your hand to me and beginning the process of restoration. I don't know where I'd be without You, and at this point, I'm not willing to find out! I'm never leaving Your side. You've proven I can trust you. And trust You, I will.

Your baby girl,

Amen.

REFERENCES

Evette, S. (Director). (2020, September 22). N.E.W. - Nothing Ever Wasted! How the trash becomes TREASURE [Video file]. Retrieved from https://www.youtube.com/watch?v=Hu1kkGD2jmY&t=383s

Made in United States
North Haven, CT
10 December 2023

45482426R00039